The Giant Book of Twisted Facts

by
Jake Jacobs

* * * * *

Published by Jake Jacobs

1.

Grevy's zebra is the largest and most distinct species of zebra, characterized by its tall stature, narrow stripes, and large ears.

2.

Named after the former French president Jules Grevy, Grevy's zebra is scientifically known as Equus grevyi.

3.

Grevy's zebras are native to semi-arid regions of East Africa, primarily found in parts of Kenya and Ethiopia.

4.

These zebras inhabit open grasslands, savannas, and shrublands, often near water sources for hydration.

5.

Grevy's zebras are easily distinguishable from other zebra species by their thin and closely spaced black and white stripes, which continue down their legs.

6.

Their large ears serve as an efficient cooling mechanism, helping to regulate their body temperature in the hot African climate.

7.

Grevy's zebras have a distinctive white underbelly, which contrasts with their darker upper body and stripes.

8.

Unlike other zebras, Grevy's zebras have a mane that stands upright, extending from their neck to their back.

9.

Adult Grevy's zebras can reach a height of about 5 to 6 feet at the shoulder and a length of around 8 to 9.5 feet from head to tail.

10.

These zebras are also the heaviest among zebra species, with males weighing around 900 to 1,000 kg (2,000 to 2,200 lbs) and females weighing slightly less.

11.

Grevy's zebras are well adapted to their arid environment and have the ability to survive without water for several days.

12.

Their diet primarily consists of coarse grasses and browsed leaves from shrubs and trees.

13.

Grevy's zebras are social animals that usually gather in small groups called "harems." Each harem is typically composed of one adult male and several females with their offspring.

14.

Adult males are highly territorial and mark their territory using urine and scent markings.

15.

During the breeding season, adult males engage in confrontations to establish dominance and access to females.

16.

Grevy's zebras have a longer gestation period compared to other equids, lasting around 13 to 14 months.

17.

Newborn Grevy's zebras, called foals, are born with brown stripes that darken over time.

18.

Foals are able to stand and walk within a few hours of birth, and they can start eating solid food within a few weeks.

19.

Grevy's zebras have a lifespan of around 20 to 25 years in the wild.

20.

The population of Grevy's zebras has significantly declined due to habitat loss, competition for resources, and poaching.

21.

Grevy's zebras are classified as endangered by the International Union for Conservation of Nature (IUCN).

22.

Conservation efforts for Grevy's zebras include habitat protection, anti-poaching measures, and community education programs.

23.

These zebras play a crucial role in their ecosystem by being seed dispersers for various plant species.

24.

Grevy's zebras use vocalizations, such as braying and barking, to communicate with one another.

25.

They also use body language, such as ear position and tail movement, to convey their emotions and intentions.

26.

Unlike other zebras, Grevy's zebras are less likely to form mixed-species groups with other herbivores.

27.

Their stripes are believed to serve as a form of camouflage, helping them blend into their environment and evade predators.

28.

Grevy's zebras are preyed upon by large carnivores such as lions, hyenas, and African wild dogs.

29.

These zebras are known for their keen sense of hearing and sight, which helps them detect predators from a distance.

30.

Grevy's zebras have a unique and intricate social structure within harems, involving various behaviors and interactions.

31.

Grevy's zebras exhibit a behavior known as "flehmen," where they curl back their lips and raise their heads to inhale scents in the air or on the ground.

32.

They are able to run at speeds of up to 40 miles per hour (65 km/h) to escape predators.

33.

Grevy's zebras have a keen memory and can recognize individual members of their social groups.

34.

Despite their size and strength, Grevy's zebras are known to be more cautious and less aggressive compared to other equids.

35.

They are well adapted to their dry environment, as their kidneys are specialized to concentrate urine and retain water.

36.

Grevy's zebras are more solitary compared to other zebra species, and they tend to roam larger home ranges.

37.

These zebras have a unique breeding call, which is a loud braying sound that helps attract mates and establish territories.

38.

Grevy's zebras have been depicted in various forms of African art and culture, symbolizing the beauty and diversity of the continent's wildlife.

39.

In addition to their natural predators, Grevy's zebras also face threats from habitat fragmentation and human development.

40.

Grevy's zebras have large, mobile lips that help them strip leaves and grasses from plants.

41.

The distinctive pattern of their stripes has been studied by scientists to understand zebra behavior and social interactions.

42.

Grevy's zebras are known to engage in mutual grooming, which helps strengthen social bonds within the harem.

43.

They are known to roll in dust or mud to help prevent insect bites and regulate body temperature.

44.

Grevy's zebras are known for their ability to adapt to various types of vegetation, which is crucial in their arid habitat.

45.

Conservation efforts for Grevy's zebras involve community-based initiatives to protect their habitats and reduce human-wildlife conflict.

46.

Grevy's zebras have a slow reproductive rate, which makes their populations vulnerable to decline.

47.

The distinctive characteristics of Grevy's zebras have made them a subject of interest for researchers and conservationists studying animal behavior and ecology.

48.

Grevy's zebras are sometimes referred to as the "royal zebra" due to their regal appearance and unique features.

49.

The survival of Grevy's zebras is essential not only for their species but also for the broader ecosystem they inhabit.

50.

By raising awareness and supporting conservation efforts, humans can contribute to the protection and preservation of Grevy's zebras and their habitat.

51.

The Grey Junglefowl is a wild ancestor of the domesticated chicken (Gallus gallus domesticus).

52.

This species was first described by French naturalist Pierre Sonnerat in 1782.

53.

The Grey Junglefowl is also known by other names, including Sonnerat's Junglefowl, Ceylon Junglefowl, and Sri Lanka Junglefowl.

54.

It is widely distributed in parts of India, Sri Lanka, and the surrounding regions.

55.

Male Grey Junglefowls are larger than females, reaching lengths of around 24 inches (60 cm) and weighing up to 3 pounds (1.4 kg).

56.

Females are generally smaller, measuring about 16 inches (40 cm) in length and weighing around 2 pounds (0.9 kg).

57.

These birds have striking blue-grey plumage on the upper parts of their body, while the underparts are a rich, warm cinnamon color.

58.

Their legs are strong and well-adapted for scratching the forest floor in search of food.

59.

Males are known for their distinctive crowing call, which is a series of loud and resonant cackles.

60.

Grey Junglefowls are known for their bold and colorful facial features, including bright red combs and wattles.

61.

They inhabit various forest types, from dry deciduous to moist evergreen forests, often at elevations ranging from sea level to about 7,000 feet (2,100 meters).

62.

These birds are omnivorous, feeding on a variety of food items such as seeds, fruits, insects, small vertebrates, and even small reptiles.

63.

Grey Junglefowls play an important role in maintaining the ecological balance by controlling insect populations and aiding in seed dispersal.

64.

Males have prominent spurs on their legs, which they use for protection and territorial disputes.

65.

During the breeding season, males engage in elaborate courtship displays to attract females. These displays include puffing up feathers, fanning the tail, and strutting.

66.

The females build simple nests on the ground, using leaves and twigs. They are usually well-concealed in the underbrush.

67.

A typical clutch size consists of 4 to 6 eggs. The eggs are creamy-white in color and may be incubated for about three weeks.

68.

Chicks are precocial, meaning they are relatively independent and can forage for food shortly after hatching.

69.

Grey Junglefowls are primarily terrestrial birds but can fly short distances if necessary.

70.

In Sri Lanka, the Grey Junglefowl is considered the national bird.

71.

The species has a significant place in traditional and cultural practices in many parts of South Asia.

72.

These birds are known for their adaptability and have managed to survive in various habitats, even in close proximity to human settlements.

73.

They are primarily diurnal, being active during the day and resting at night.

74.

Grey Junglefowls are social birds, often seen in small groups or pairs.

75.

In some regions, Grey Junglefowls are considered a game bird and are hunted for meat.

76.

They have a relatively long lifespan in the wild, averaging around 10 to 15 years.

77.

The Grey Junglefowl's natural habitat is under threat due to deforestation, habitat loss, and fragmentation.

78.

They are considered near threatened by the International Union for Conservation of Nature (IUCN) due to these threats and hunting pressures.

79.

Conservation efforts are ongoing to protect the Grey Junglefowl and its habitat.

80.

Hybridization with domesticated chickens has been identified as a potential threat to the genetic purity of the species.

81.

The Grey Junglefowl's scientific name, Gallus sonneratii, honors the French naturalist Pierre Sonnerat, who first described the species.

82.

They have a strong association with Hindu mythology and are often depicted in various ancient texts.

83.

Grey Junglefowls have been celebrated for their vibrant plumage and have inspired various art forms.

84.

These birds are excellent runners and use their strong legs to swiftly navigate through the undergrowth.

85.

Their diet varies based on availability and can include grains, fruits, insects, and small vertebrates.

86.

Grey Junglefowls often take dust baths to help keep their plumage clean and free of parasites.

87.

In some regions, they have been observed roosting in trees to avoid ground predators.

88.

These birds are known for their alert nature and will quickly disappear into the underbrush at the slightest hint of danger.

89.

The distinctive crowing of the males can be heard early in the morning, serving as a territorial call.

90.

Grey Junglefowls have played a role in scientific research on avian genetics and behavior.

91.

They are also important seed dispersers for various plant species, contributing to forest regeneration.

92.

These birds exhibit a strong sense of hierarchy within social groups.

93.

Habitat restoration and protected areas are crucial for the long-term survival of the Grey Junglefowl.

94.

The Grey Junglefowl is part of the Galliformes order, which also includes pheasants, quails, and turkeys.

95.

They have relatively large eyes that provide them with good vision, helping them detect predators from a distance.

96.

Despite their wild nature, Grey Junglefowls have adapted to living in close proximity to human settlements.

97.

These birds are often depicted in traditional Indian art, literature, and cultural festivals.

98.

The loss of their natural habitat can lead to increased human-wildlife conflicts as they search for food and shelter.

99.

Captive breeding programs have been initiated to help conserve and reintroduce Grey Junglefowls into the wild.

100.

Appreciating and understanding the Grey Junglefowl's ecological role and cultural significance is essential for its long-term survival and protection.

101.

MGM Resorts International was founded on August 29, 1986, as MGM Grand, Inc.

102.

The company's original headquarters was located in Las Vegas, Nevada.

103.

The iconic MGM Grand Hotel and Casino in Las Vegas, known for its distinctive green color, served as the flagship property for the company.

104.

MGM Resorts was initially formed as a merger between Kerkorian's MGM Grand and Bally Entertainment Corporation.

105.

The company's founder, Kirk Kerkorian, was a prominent businessman and investor who played a significant role in the development of the Las Vegas Strip.

106.

The company changed its name to MGM Mirage in 2000, reflecting its broadened portfolio beyond the MGM Grand property.

107.

MGM Mirage acquired several other renowned properties, including Bellagio, Mirage, and Treasure Island, cementing its status as a major player in the hospitality and entertainment industry.

108.

In 2004, MGM Mirage completed the acquisition of Mandalay Resort Group, further expanding its presence on the Las Vegas Strip.

109.

MGM Resorts played a pivotal role in revitalizing the city of Detroit with the opening of the MGM Grand Detroit casino in 2007.

110.

The company's expansion wasn't limited to the United States; it also ventured into international markets. MGM Macau opened in 2007, marking its entry into the Asian gaming market.

111.

In 2009, MGM Mirage faced financial challenges due to the global economic recession. It engaged in significant restructuring efforts to address its debt.

112.

As part of its reorganization, MGM Mirage sold its Treasure Island property in 2009 to help reduce its debt burden.

113.

MGM Resorts launched its M Life Rewards program, a loyalty program that offers members various benefits and experiences across its properties.

114.

MGM Resorts was involved in the development of CityCenter, a massive mixed-use complex on the Las Vegas Strip that includes hotels, residences, and a shopping center.

115.

Aria Resort & Casino, one of the key properties within CityCenter, opened its doors in 2009 and quickly became a prominent Las Vegas destination.

116.

The company continued its international expansion with the opening of MGM Cotai in Macau in 2018.

117.

In 2010, MGM Mirage officially changed its name to MGM Resorts International to better reflect its global reach and diverse portfolio.

118.

MGM Resorts is known for its commitment to sustainability and environmental responsibility. Its CityCenter complex in Las Vegas was designed with eco-friendly features.

119.

The company's Mandalay Bay property in Las Vegas hosted the Route 91 Harvest music festival in 2017, which tragically became the site of the deadliest mass shooting in modern American history.

120.

MGM Resorts initiated the Universal Love album project in 2018, which featured reimagined versions of iconic songs with LGBTQ themes.

121.

The company has a strong presence in entertainment, including hosting major events, concerts, and performances at its various properties.

122.

MGM Resorts International established the MGM Resorts Foundation, a charitable organization that supports various causes and initiatives.

123.

The Bellagio Conservatory and Botanical Gardens at the Bellagio Las Vegas property is renowned for its elaborate seasonal displays and attracts millions of visitors annually.

124.

The company's portfolio includes properties in several US states, including Nevada, Michigan, New Jersey, and Mississippi.

125.

MGM Resorts International has consistently been recognized for its commitment to diversity and inclusion.

126.

The company has been involved in various philanthropic efforts, supporting organizations and initiatives focused on education, health, and community development.

127.

MGM Resorts is a key partner in the Las Vegas community, contributing to local organizations and events.

128.

The company played a crucial role in the development of the T-Mobile Arena on the Las Vegas Strip, which hosts major concerts, sporting events, and entertainment shows.

<h1 style="text-align:center">129.</h1>

MGM Resorts is a significant employer in Las Vegas and other cities, providing thousands of jobs in the hospitality and entertainment sectors.

<h1 style="text-align:center">130.</h1>

The company has a history of collaborating with celebrities and artists for various projects and events.

<h1 style="text-align:center">131.</h1>

MGM Resorts has been recognized for its commitment to responsible gaming and initiatives to address problem gambling.

<h1 style="text-align:center">132.</h1>

The company has made efforts to enhance its digital and online presence, providing customers with a seamless experience across platforms.

<h1 style="text-align:center">133.</h1>

MGM Resorts' properties are known for their luxurious accommodations, world-class dining options, and high-quality entertainment offerings.

<h1 style="text-align:center">134.</h1>

In 2016, MGM Resorts International completed the acquisition of Borgata Hotel Casino & Spa in Atlantic City, further expanding its East Coast presence.

<h1 style="text-align:center">135.</h1>

The company launched the Park MGM concept in Las Vegas, focusing on creating a unique urban oasis with outdoor spaces and dining options.

136.

The Park MGM property is home to the T-Mobile Arena and the Park Theater, which hosts performances by top artists and entertainers.

137.

MGM Resorts is known for its commitment to innovation, including exploring new technologies and trends in the hospitality industry.

138.

The company has taken steps to reduce its environmental footprint by implementing energy-efficient practices and sustainability initiatives.

139.

MGM Resorts International's properties often feature impressive art installations and collections, contributing to the overall guest experience.

140.

The company's commitment to employee development and training has earned it recognition as an employer of choice.

141.

MGM Resorts has embraced virtual reality and other immersive technologies to enhance guest experiences and attract new audiences.

142.

The company has been involved in the construction and expansion of various convention and meeting spaces to cater to business travelers.

143.

MGM Resorts International has demonstrated resilience in the face of challenges, including economic downturns and shifts in consumer preferences.

144.

The company has made strides in enhancing accessibility and inclusivity for guests with disabilities.

145.

MGM Resorts is actively engaged in efforts to support responsible tourism and protect the environment in destinations where it operates.

146.

The company has been recognized for its commitment to corporate social responsibility and ethical business practices.

147.

MGM Resorts has contributed to the development of innovative entertainment concepts, including immersive theater experiences and interactive exhibits.

148.

The company's commitment to entertainment extends to its sponsorship of major events, including awards shows and sporting events.

149.

MGM Resorts has been recognized for its efforts in promoting gender equality and women's leadership within the organization.

150.

Throughout its history, MGM Resorts International has remained a prominent player in the hospitality and entertainment industry,

continually evolving to meet the changing preferences of guests and
consumers.

151.

DuPont was founded in 1802 by Éleuthère Irénée du Pont, a French
chemist, and gunpowder manufacturer.

152.

The company's first product was gunpowder, which quickly gained a
reputation for its quality and reliability.

153.

During the War of 1812, DuPont supplied gunpowder to the United
States military, solidifying its role as a significant supplier of
munitions.

154.

DuPont played a crucial role in introducing the modern industrial
research laboratory model, focusing on innovation and scientific
advancement.

155.

The company's headquarters is located in Wilmington, Delaware,
where it has remained for over two centuries.

156.

In the 19th century, DuPont expanded its product range to include a
variety of chemicals, dyes, and other industrial materials.

157.

DuPont introduced the "Chemists' War Service" during World War I,
where the company's expertise was utilized to develop military
technologies.

158.

The company's research efforts led to the development of synthetic materials like neoprene, nylon, and Teflon, significantly impacting various industries.

159.

DuPont's nylon was introduced in the 1930s and quickly became a sensation, revolutionizing the textile and fashion industries.

160.

During World War II, DuPont contributed to the war effort by developing products like synthetic rubber and parachutes.

161.

In 1950, DuPont introduced Dacron, a synthetic polyester fiber that found applications in textiles, packaging, and more.

162.

Teflon, introduced in the 1940s, became widely known for its nonstick properties and found use in cookware and various industrial applications.

163.

The company played a crucial role in the development of the Manhattan Project, contributing materials used in the construction of atomic bombs.

164.

DuPont was involved in the production of Freon, a chlorofluorocarbon (CFC) compound used in refrigeration systems, until concerns about its environmental impact arose.

165.

In 1981, DuPont introduced Lycra, a synthetic fiber that revolutionized the comfort and stretchiness of fabrics.

166.

The company's focus on safety and environmental responsibility led to the development of the Responsible Care initiative in the 1980s.

167.

In the 1990s, DuPont faced controversy over the environmental impact of perfluorooctanoic acid (PFOA), an ingredient used in Teflon production.

168.

In 1999, DuPont spun off its chemical division, creating the independent company, The Chemours Company.

169.

DuPont's acquisition of Conoco in 1981 expanded its presence in the energy sector.

170.

The company established the DuPont Experimental Station in Wilmington, which became a center for scientific research and innovation.

171.

DuPont's involvement in agriculture led to the development of genetically modified crops and seeds resistant to pests and herbicides.

172.

The company played a significant role in the development of biofuels as an alternative to traditional fossil fuels.

173.

DuPont's expertise in advanced materials has led to innovations in the aerospace, automotive, and electronics industries.

174.

DuPont's involvement in the development of Kevlar, a high-strength synthetic fiber, has saved countless lives by providing protection in various applications, including bulletproof vests.

175.

The company's acquisition of Pioneer Hi-Bred International in 1999 expanded its presence in the agricultural biotechnology sector.

176.

DuPont's focus on sustainability led to the creation of environmentally friendly products and processes.

177.

The company played a key role in the development of photovoltaic materials for solar panels.

178.

In 2015, DuPont announced its merger with The Dow Chemical Company, forming DowDuPont.

179.

The merger was followed by the subsequent separation of DowDuPont into three independent companies: Dow Inc., Corteva Agriscience, and DuPont.

180.

In 2019, DuPont officially became known as DuPont de Nemours, Inc., emphasizing its legacy and heritage.

181.

The company continues to be a leader in the development of innovative materials for various industries, including electronics and healthcare.

182.

DuPont's commitment to diversity and inclusion has earned it recognition as an employer of choice.

183.

The company has consistently ranked on lists of the world's most admired companies and sustainable corporations.

184.

DuPont has a history of philanthropy, supporting education, community development, and environmental initiatives.

185.

DuPont's iconic oval logo, designed in 1906, is one of the oldest and most recognizable corporate logos.

186.

The company's commitment to safety has led to the implementation of rigorous safety protocols and practices.

187.

DuPont's innovations have contributed to advancements in medical devices, enabling the development of safer and more effective healthcare solutions.

188.

The company's products have been used in various space missions, contributing to advancements in space exploration.

189.

DuPont's role in developing fire-resistant materials has been crucial for improving the safety of firefighters and military personnel.

190.

The company has been recognized for its contributions to sustainability and environmental stewardship.

191.

DuPont's involvement in agriculture includes the development of crop protection solutions and sustainable farming practices.

192.

The company's expertise in polymer science has led to innovations in packaging materials, enhancing the shelf life of products and reducing food waste.

193.

DuPont has a long history of collaboration with other industry leaders, fostering innovation and knowledge sharing.

194.

The company's commitment to research and development has led to a vast portfolio of patents and intellectual property.

195.

DuPont's technologies have been applied to various industries, including construction, automotive, electronics, and consumer goods.

196.

The DuPont Oval Room, located in the Hagley Museum and Library, showcases the company's history and innovations.

197.

The company has faced challenges and controversies over the years, addressing concerns related to environmental impact and worker safety.

198.

DuPont's legacy of innovation continues to influence the scientific and technological landscape of the 21st century.

199.

The company's commitment to sustainability and responsible practices has positioned it as a leader in the movement towards a more sustainable future.

200.

DuPont de Nemours, Inc., continues to drive progress through innovation, research, and a dedication to creating solutions for a better world.

201.

The L.A. Dunton is a two-masted fishing schooner, designed and built in 1921 by Thomas F. McManus in Essex, Massachusetts.

202.

It was named after Lawrence A. Dunton, a prominent fisherman and merchant from Gloucester, Massachusetts.

203.

The schooner was constructed using traditional shipbuilding methods, with a wooden hull made of oak and pine.

204.

L.A. Dunton was primarily used for commercial fishing, especially for the Gloucester fishing fleet during the peak of the Grand Banks fishing industry.

205.

The vessel was designed to withstand the harsh conditions of the North Atlantic, known for its unpredictable weather and rough seas.

206.

L.A. Dunton was employed in various types of fishing, including cod, halibut, and mackerel, contributing to the economy of the New England fishing industry.

207.

The schooner's design and construction incorporated both traditional fishing techniques and modern advancements of the early 20th century.

208.

L.A. Dunton's hull design featured a distinctive clipper bow, a characteristic of many fishing vessels of that era.

209.

The vessel's two-masted rigging allowed it to carry a variety of sails for different wind conditions, enhancing its versatility.

210.

L.A. Dunton was also equipped with an auxiliary engine, marking a transition from purely sail-powered vessels to those with hybrid propulsion systems.

211.

The schooner played a critical role in sustaining the fishing communities along the New England coast.

212.

During its operational years, L.A. Dunton participated in the International Fishermen's Race, a friendly competition among fishing schooners.

213.

The vessel's participation in races showcased its speed, agility, and the skills of its crew.

214.

L.A. Dunton underwent several modifications and repairs over the years to adapt to changing fishing techniques and regulations.

215.

The schooner experienced the decline of the fishing industry in the mid-20th century, leading to a decrease in its commercial use.

216.

In the 1960s, L.A. Dunton was retired from active fishing and faced the risk of deterioration and neglect.

217.

Recognizing its historical significance, the vessel was acquired by Mystic Seaport Museum in Mystic, Connecticut, in 1963.

218.

The museum embarked on a meticulous restoration project to bring L.A. Dunton back to its original condition.

219.

The restoration involved extensive research, documentation, and collaboration with experts in maritime history and shipbuilding.

220.

L.A. Dunton's restoration showcased the dedication of craftsmen and preservationists in reviving a piece of maritime heritage.

221.

The restored schooner became a part of Mystic Seaport's collection of historic vessels, allowing visitors to experience the maritime past firsthand.

222.

L.A. Dunton serves as an educational platform, offering visitors insights into the life of fishermen, the history of fishing, and traditional shipbuilding techniques.

223.

The vessel's interior and deck are furnished with equipment, tools, and artifacts that reflect the working environment of a fishing schooner.

224.

Visitors to Mystic Seaport have the opportunity to explore L.A. Dunton and gain a deeper understanding of the challenges faced by seafarers.

225.

L.A. Dunton is often used for educational programs, sailing excursions, and special events, providing an immersive experience for visitors of all ages.

226.

The schooner's restoration received recognition for its commitment to preserving maritime history and craftsmanship.

227.

L.A. Dunton's presence at Mystic Seaport contributes to the museum's mission of promoting maritime education and preserving maritime heritage.

228.

The vessel's participation in maritime festivals and events helps raise awareness about the importance of preserving historical vessels.

229.

The schooner's design and construction showcase the ingenuity of shipbuilders in the early 20th century, combining tradition with technological advancements.

230.

L.A. Dunton's iconic appearance and history have made it a subject of fascination for maritime enthusiasts and historians.

231.

The vessel's story is intertwined with the evolution of fishing practices, shipbuilding techniques, and maritime commerce.

232.

L.A. Dunton represents the enduring legacy of New England's fishing heritage, paying tribute to the men and women who worked on similar vessels.

233.

The schooner's restoration required the collaboration of various skilled artisans, from shipwrights to riggers and sailmakers.

234.

L.A. Dunton's historical significance extends beyond its role in fishing; it reflects broader societal changes during its operational years.

235.

The vessel's design and construction incorporate elements of both utility and aesthetics, reflecting the craftsmanship of its builders.

236.

L.A. Dunton's presence at Mystic Seaport allows visitors to step back in time and experience life aboard a working fishing schooner.

237.

The restoration of L.A. Dunton emphasizes the importance of preserving tangible links to maritime history for future generations.

238.

The schooner's participation in maritime festivals and regattas contributes to the vibrant maritime culture and heritage of New England.

239.

L.A. Dunton's restoration project required extensive research to ensure historical accuracy in every aspect of the vessel's design.

240.

The vessel's historical documentation, including photographs and records, played a crucial role in guiding the restoration process.

241.

The restoration process included sourcing appropriate materials and recreating traditional shipbuilding techniques to ensure authenticity.

242.

L.A. Dunton's restoration stands as a testament to the dedication and passion of those who work to preserve maritime history.

243.

The schooner's enduring presence at Mystic Seaport serves as a reminder of the vital role that fishing vessels played in shaping coastal communities.

244.

L.A. Dunton's history embodies the stories of seafarers, fishermen, and their families who depended on such vessels for their livelihoods.

245.

The vessel's sailing excursions offer visitors a unique opportunity to experience the thrill of being on board a historic schooner.

246.

L.A. Dunton's restoration highlights the importance of maritime museums and organizations in safeguarding maritime heritage.

247.

The vessel's restoration process aimed to strike a balance between preserving historical authenticity and ensuring visitor safety.

248.

L.A. Dunton's wooden hull and rigging represent the craftsmanship of a bygone era when ships were intricately constructed by hand.

249.

The schooner's legacy continues to inspire discussions about the significance of maritime history in understanding our cultural heritage.

250.

L.A. Dunton's story serves as a reminder of the human connection to the sea and the enduring impact of maritime traditions on our lives.

251.

The Litchfield Historic District is located in Litchfield, Connecticut, and encompasses approximately 1,550 acres of land.

252.

It was designated a National Historic Landmark in 1969, recognizing its exceptional architectural and historical significance.

253.

The district includes more than 240 historically significant structures, making it one of the largest historic districts in Connecticut.

254.

Litchfield was established in 1719 and is known for its well-preserved New England architecture from the 18th and 19th centuries.

255.

The district showcases a variety of architectural styles, including Colonial, Federal, Greek Revival, and Victorian.

256.

Litchfield's Main Street is lined with beautifully preserved houses and buildings that reflect the town's prosperous history.

257.

The district includes the Tapping Reeve House and Law School, founded by Tapping Reeve in 1774, which is considered the first law school in the United States.

258.

The Litchfield Female Academy, founded in 1792 by Sarah Pierce, was one of the earliest institutions of higher learning for women in the United States.

259.

The district also features the Litchfield Historical Society, which plays a significant role in preserving and interpreting the town's history.

260.

The Oliver Wolcott House, a grand Federal-style mansion, was the home of Oliver Wolcott Jr., a signer of the Declaration of Independence.

261.

The district includes the Congregational Church of Litchfield, a beautiful example of Federal-style architecture with a towering white steeple.

262.

The Litchfield Inn, a historic hotel dating back to the 18th century, offers visitors a glimpse into the town's hospitality and charm.

263.

The Litchfield County Jail, built in 1812, features an octagonal design and is one of the earliest examples of its kind in the United States.

264.

The district's landscapes include picturesque streetscapes, lush gardens, and well-maintained public spaces.

265.

Litchfield was a hub of intellectual and cultural activity in the 18th and 19th centuries, attracting scholars, writers, and artists.

266.

Famous figures such as Harriet Beecher Stowe, Henry Ward Beecher, and John C. Calhoun have connections to Litchfield.

267.

The district's architecture reflects the changing tastes and trends of different time periods, providing a visual timeline of American history.

268.

Litchfield's historic district offers walking tours that allow visitors to explore its streets, landmarks, and fascinating stories.

269.

The Litchfield Historical Society's museum exhibits offer a comprehensive overview of the town's history, culture, and notable residents.

270.

Litchfield's residential architecture showcases a mix of single-family homes, grand estates, and smaller cottages.

271.

The district's well-preserved buildings have been used as filming locations for various movies and TV shows set in the 18th and 19th centuries.

272.

The architecture and streetscapes of the Litchfield Historic District have served as inspirations for artists, painters, and writers.

273.

The district's inclusion of educational institutions like the Litchfield Law School and the Female Academy highlights its role in shaping American education.

274.

The district's architectural diversity includes examples of brick, wood, and stone construction, showcasing different building materials of the time.

275.

Some of the historic buildings in the district have been converted into bed-and-breakfast establishments, offering visitors a unique lodging experience.

276.

The Litchfield Historical Society offers programs and events that celebrate the town's history, culture, and architectural heritage.

277.

Litchfield's history is closely tied to the development of New England's early legal, educational, and religious institutions.

278.

The district's architectural details include intricate woodwork, decorative moldings, and classic New England features like dormer windows.

279.

The district's landscapes showcase well-maintained lawns, gardens, and pathways that invite visitors to explore on foot.

280.

Litchfield's historic district attracts visitors interested in history, architecture, preservation, and the stories of early American life.

281.

The Litchfield Historical Society maintains an extensive collection of artifacts, documents, and archives related to the town's history.

282.

The district's historic buildings are often privately owned and well-maintained by residents who take pride in preserving their town's heritage.

283.

Litchfield's significance extends beyond its architecture; its role in American history includes contributions to politics, law, and education.

284.

The district's buildings have been meticulously restored to their original appearances, ensuring their historical accuracy.

285.

The Litchfield Historical Society hosts educational programs for schools, offering students an opportunity to learn about local history firsthand.

286.

The district's preservation efforts have helped maintain the town's unique character and sense of place.

287.

Litchfield's architecture reflects the lifestyle and aspirations of its early residents, providing insights into their values and priorities.

288.

The district's buildings often feature traditional New England colors, such as white clapboard siding and black shutters.

289.

The Tapping Reeve House and Law School offers guided tours that provide insight into early legal education and life in the 18th century.

290.

The Litchfield Historical Society's library and research center offer resources for scholars, researchers, and those interested in genealogy.

291.

Litchfield's historic district serves as a model for successful preservation efforts and community engagement.

292.

The district's architecture exemplifies the craftsmanship and attention to detail that defined early American construction methods.

293.

Litchfield's role in shaping American education and legal systems is celebrated through exhibitions, lectures, and educational programs.

294.

The district's buildings reflect the influence of different architectural styles, including Georgian, Federal, and Greek Revival.

295.

The Litchfield Historical Society collaborates with local schools to integrate history into the curriculum and engage students in learning.

296.

The district's preservation efforts have been supported by organizations, volunteers, and community members dedicated to safeguarding its heritage.

297.

Litchfield's historical landmarks provide a glimpse into the lives of early settlers, merchants, educators, and other notable figures.

298.

The district's preservation efforts have helped attract heritage tourism, benefiting the local economy and fostering a sense of pride among residents.

299.

Litchfield's Main Street is often recognized as one of the most charming and well-preserved streetscapes in New England.

300.

The Litchfield Historic District is a testament to the town's enduring commitment to preserving its architectural and cultural heritage for future generations.

301.

The Grey Go-away-bird gets its name from its distinctive call, which sounds like it's saying "go away" or "grey loerie."

302.

It belongs to the turaco family, which is a group of colorful birds known for their vibrant plumage and unique vocalizations.

303.

The Grey Loerie is predominantly grey in color, with shades ranging from light gray to charcoal, and it has a white belly.

304.

It has a distinctive black mask around its eyes, which gives it a unique and striking appearance.

305.

The bird has a long, graduated tail and a distinctive, forward-curving crest on its head.

306.

Grey Loeries are medium-sized birds, measuring around 44 to 50 cm (17 to 20 inches) in length.

307.

They have strong, hooked bills that are well adapted for feeding on fruit and leaves.

308.

These birds are known for their distinctive, noisy calls, which can be heard echoing through the forests and woodlands where they live.

309.

Grey Loeries are monogamous and form strong pair bonds that last throughout the breeding season.

310.

They are mainly frugivorous, meaning their diet primarily consists of fruits, especially figs and berries.

311.

In addition to fruit, they also feed on leaves, flowers, and even some insects.

312.

Grey Loeries are known to occasionally forage on the ground for fallen fruits.

313.

These birds are important seed dispersers in their habitats, helping to maintain the diversity of plant species.

314.

They are often found in savannas, woodlands, and forests across sub-Saharan Africa.

315.

Grey Loeries are agile and skilled fliers, with strong wingbeats and the ability to glide gracefully between trees.

316.

They are known for their distinct and elaborate courtship displays, which involve bowing, preening, and mutual feeding between mates.

317.

Their nests are often constructed in the fork of a tree, using twigs and branches lined with leaves.

318.

The female Grey Loerie typically lays 1 to 3 eggs per clutch.

319.

Both parents take turns incubating the eggs, which hatch after about 24 to 25 days.

320.

The chicks are born helpless and are cared for by their parents until they are able to fledge.

321.

Grey Loeries are known for their strong territorial behavior, and they can be aggressive in defending their feeding and nesting areas.

322.

They are generally shy and elusive birds, often hiding among foliage to avoid detection.

323.

Grey Loeries are also known to emit a series of hisses and whistles when threatened or disturbed.

324.

These birds are often seen in small groups or pairs, although they can also be solitary.

325.

Grey Loeries are important indicators of the health of forest ecosystems due to their role in seed dispersal.

326.

The Grey Loerie's scientific name, Corythaixoides concolor, reflects its resemblance to both the turaco and the go-away-bird.

327.

They are considered to be culturally important in some African communities and are sometimes associated with superstitions and beliefs.

328.

In certain regions, Grey Loeries are hunted for their meat and feathers.

329.

Their feathers are sometimes used for traditional adornments and rituals.

330.

Grey Loeries have been observed engaging in sunbathing behavior, spreading their wings and exposing their bellies to the sun.

331.

These birds have a strong presence in African folklore and are often included in stories and myths.

332.

They are also commonly referred to as "Lourie" or "Touraco" in various African languages.

333.

In some areas, Grey Loeries are considered pests due to their fondness for cultivated fruits.

334.

The Grey Loerie's flight is characterized by deep, steady wingbeats.

335.

Despite their size, they are known for their agility and the ease with which they maneuver through the dense vegetation.

336.

Grey Loeries have a slow and deliberate manner of walking on branches and among leaves.

337.

They have a unique vocal repertoire that includes a range of calls, from their signature "go away" call to soft cooing sounds.

338.

Their vocalizations are often used to communicate with their mate and defend their territory.

339.

The Grey Loerie's plumage provides excellent camouflage among the tree branches and leaves.

340.

Their diet can vary depending on the season and availability of food sources.

341.

These birds are excellent climbers and often move through the trees using a combination of hopping and clambering.

342.

Grey Loeries have strong legs and feet, which are adapted for perching on branches and grasping fruits.

343.

They are known to engage in mutual preening behaviors with their mates, which helps strengthen their bond.

344.

Grey Loeries are considered to be one of the more iconic and recognizable birds in African birdwatching.

345.

Their presence in local ecosystems contributes to the overall biodiversity and ecological balance.

346.

These birds play a role in controlling insect populations through their consumption of insects and other invertebrates.

347.

The Grey Loerie is also known by various other names, including Gray Go-away-bird and Grey Lourie.

348.

They are well-adapted to life in the treetops, rarely descending to the ground.

349.

Grey Loeries are sometimes kept in captivity as ornamental birds due to their striking appearance and distinctive calls.

350.

These birds have captured the fascination of bird enthusiasts and researchers alike, contributing to our understanding of avian behavior and ecology in African ecosystems.

351.

The Grey Partridge is a medium-sized game bird belonging to the Phasianidae family.

352.

It is also commonly referred to as the English Partridge or simply the "grey."

353.

The bird's scientific name, Perdix perdix, is derived from the Latin word "perdix," which means partridge.

354.

Grey Partridges are known for their distinctive call, a repeated "kerrr-ik" sound that is often heard during their breeding season.

355.

They have a plump, rounded body with a short tail, giving them a compact and sturdy appearance.

356.

The bird's plumage is predominantly gray, which provides excellent camouflage in their natural habitat.

357.

Males and females have similar coloration, but males often have a brighter white face with a horseshoe-shaped patch.

358.

Grey Partridges have chestnut-colored bellies and distinctive orange-brown facial markings.

359.

They are ground-dwelling birds and are well adapted for running rather than flying to escape predators.

360.

Their wings are broad and rounded, allowing for quick takeoffs and short flights.

361.

The species is known for its strong flying ability and can fly for relatively long distances when necessary.

362.

Grey Partridges are often found in agricultural landscapes, grasslands, and open fields.

363.

They are widely distributed across Europe and parts of western Asia.

364.

The diet of Grey Partridges primarily consists of seeds, grains, and insects.

365.

These birds are known to feed on a variety of plants, including cereal crops, weeds, and grasses.

366.

The Grey Partridge's nest is a simple ground scrape lined with vegetation, hidden in dense vegetation or tall grasses.

367.

The female typically lays around 10 to 20 eggs in a single clutch.

368.

Both the male and female take turns incubating the eggs, which hatch after about three weeks.

369.

The chicks are precocial, meaning they are born with their eyes open and are able to feed themselves shortly after hatching.

370.

Grey Partridges are known for their strong parental care, and parents will protect and guide their chicks to food and cover.

371.

They often forage in family groups, with the chicks learning essential survival skills from their parents.

372.

The species has faced declines in some areas due to habitat loss, changes in agricultural practices, and hunting pressure.

373.

Grey Partridges are commonly hunted as game birds, and their populations are managed to ensure sustainable hunting.

374.

Conservation efforts are ongoing to maintain and restore their populations through habitat management and predator control.

375.

Grey Partridges are a flagship species for promoting agri-environmental practices that benefit both wildlife and agriculture.

376.

The birds are known for forming loose flocks during the winter months for better protection and finding food.

377.

Their distinctive "kerrr-ik" calls are used to communicate with other members of their group and establish territory boundaries.

378.

Grey Partridges have strong social bonds and are often seen engaging in social interactions within their groups.

379.

These birds have been introduced to various parts of North America, although their success as established populations has been limited.

380.

In their native range, Grey Partridges have inspired cultural and folkloric associations due to their presence in agricultural landscapes.

381.

The species has a relatively short lifespan, usually living up to 2 to 3 years in the wild.

382.

The Grey Partridge's numbers can fluctuate greatly from year to year due to variations in food availability and predation.

383.

Conservationists often work with farmers to implement habitat improvements that benefit Grey Partridges and other wildlife.

384.

The birds are ground-nesting species, making them vulnerable to predation by mammals and birds of prey.

385.

They are known to take dust baths, which help maintain the health of their plumage and remove parasites.

386.

Grey Partridges have excellent vision, which aids them in detecting potential threats.

387.

The species has a relatively low reproductive rate, with some clutches failing due to predation or unfavorable weather conditions.

388.

Their adaptability to agricultural landscapes has contributed to their cultural significance in farming communities.

389.

Grey Partridges have been featured in literature and art as symbols of rural life and the changing seasons.

390.

The loss of hedgerows and grasslands in some regions has led to declines in Grey Partridge populations.

391.

Efforts to protect and enhance their habitats often involve planting hedgerows, creating buffer zones, and promoting sustainable farming practices.

392.

In some cultures, the Grey Partridge is associated with fertility and abundance due to its ability to reproduce rapidly in suitable habitats.

393.

The species' ability to thrive in farmland ecosystems makes them important indicators of overall ecosystem health.

394.

Grey Partridges are sensitive to changes in their environment, making them valuable subjects for ecological research.

395.

Their adaptability and ability to persist in human-altered landscapes have allowed them to remain present in many rural areas.

396.

Grey Partridges are sometimes used as biological control agents for agricultural pests, as they consume a variety of insects.

397.

Habitat restoration efforts for Grey Partridges often involve planting native grasses and creating diverse vegetation cover.

398.

The decline of traditional farming practices, such as crop rotations and fallow fields, has contributed to habitat loss for these birds.

399.

Organizations and conservationists work to raise awareness about the importance of preserving grasslands for Grey Partridges and other wildlife.

400.

The Grey Partridge's unique ecological role as both a game bird and an indicator of habitat health highlights the complex relationship between humans and the environment.

401.

Prudential Financial, commonly known as Prudential, is a multinational financial services company headquartered in Newark, New Jersey, USA.

402.

It was founded on May 24, 1875, by John F. Dryden in Newark, New Jersey, under the name "The Widows and Orphans Friendly Society."

403.

The company's initial purpose was to provide affordable life insurance to working-class individuals and their families.

404.

The company's first policy was issued to a teacher named Elijah Upjohn.

405.

Prudential adopted its current name, "The Prudential Insurance Company of America," in 1877.

406.

Prudential played a significant role in providing life insurance coverage to American soldiers during World War I.

407.

In the early 20th century, Prudential expanded its offerings to include industrial insurance policies, which provided small amounts of coverage to low-income individuals.

408.

The iconic "Rock of Gibraltar" logo was introduced by Prudential in the late 19th century, symbolizing strength, stability, and security.

409.

In 1909, Prudential became the first company in the United States to offer group life insurance, which provided coverage to groups of employees.

410.

The company continued to expand internationally, opening offices in London in 1879 and Japan in 1971.

411.

In 1986, Prudential entered the asset management business by creating Prudential Investment Management.

412.

Prudential demutualized and became a publicly traded company in 2001, listed on the New York Stock Exchange under the ticker symbol "PRU."

413.

The company operates through various subsidiaries, including Prudential Insurance, Prudential Retirement, Prudential Annuities, and PGIM (Prudential Global Investment Management).

414.

Prudential is one of the largest life insurance companies in the United States, providing various insurance products and financial services.

415.

The company has a strong focus on retirement planning and offers a range of retirement solutions, including annuities and retirement income products.

416.

Prudential played a role in popularizing the use of life insurance as a means of wealth transfer and estate planning.

417.

The Prudential Tower in Boston, completed in 1964, was once the tallest building in New England.

418.

The company has been involved in various philanthropic initiatives, including supporting education, healthcare, and disaster relief efforts.

419.

Prudential has received recognition for its commitment to diversity and inclusion, being included in lists like the DiversityInc Top 50 Companies for Diversity.

420.

During the Great Depression, Prudential provided financial stability to policyholders, even during challenging economic times.

421.

Prudential was one of the first insurers to offer term life insurance policies, which provided coverage for a specified term rather than a lifetime.

422.

The company's financial strength and stability have earned it high credit ratings from major credit rating agencies.

423.

In 2012, Prudential acquired the individual life insurance business of The Hartford Financial Services Group.

424.

Prudential offers a wide range of insurance products, including life insurance, disability insurance, long-term care insurance, and more.

425.

The company's motto, "Let Prudential be your rock," reflects its commitment to providing financial security to its customers.

426.

Prudential has a long history of promoting financial literacy and education through various community programs.

427.

The company has been recognized for its environmental sustainability efforts, including initiatives to reduce its carbon footprint.

428.

Prudential has expanded its operations beyond insurance, offering investment management, retirement solutions, and employee benefits services.

429.

Prudential's global footprint includes operations in Asia, Europe, Latin America, and other regions.

430.

The company has often been featured on lists of Fortune 500 companies, reflecting its significant presence in the financial services industry.

431.

Prudential's innovative products have contributed to the evolution of the insurance and financial services industry.

432.

The company's customer-centric approach has helped it build strong relationships with policyholders and clients.

433.

Prudential's philanthropic efforts include supporting initiatives that address social and economic challenges in communities around the world.

434.

The company's commitment to responsible investing led to the creation of the Prudential Sustainable Investment Leadership Fund.

435.

In 2020, Prudential acquired Assurance IQ, a technology-driven insurance platform, to enhance its digital capabilities.

436.

Prudential has adapted to changing consumer preferences by offering online and digital services to its customers.

437.

The company's commitment to diversity and inclusion extends to its workforce and leadership, fostering a culture of equality.

438.

Prudential has been involved in numerous corporate social responsibility initiatives, including financial literacy programs for underserved communities.

439.

The Prudential Center, a sports and entertainment arena in Newark, New Jersey, is named after the company.

440.

Over the years, Prudential has been recognized with awards and accolades for its ethical practices and commitment to corporate responsibility.

441.

The company's corporate governance practices emphasize transparency, accountability, and ethical conduct.

442.

Prudential has been a leader in advocating for improved retirement savings options and financial security for individuals.

443.

The company's longevity and success are attributed to its ability to adapt to changing market conditions and customer needs.

444.

Prudential's commitment to innovation is reflected in its ongoing efforts to develop new products and services that meet evolving customer demands.

445.

The company's global presence has allowed it to tap into diverse markets and cultures, tailoring its offerings to local needs.

446.

Prudential's financial advisors and planners provide personalized guidance to help individuals and families achieve their financial goals.

447.

The company's research and insights on retirement, investing, and financial planning are valuable resources for consumers.

448.

Prudential's involvement in public policy discussions has contributed to conversations about retirement security and financial well-being.

449.

The company's history is intertwined with the broader evolution of the insurance industry and its role in society.

450.

Prudential's legacy as a trusted financial partner and provider of security continues to shape its mission to help individuals and families achieve financial freedom.

451.

Northrop Grumman Corporation is a global aerospace and defense technology company headquartered in Falls Church, Virginia, USA.

452.

The company was formed through the merger of Northrop Corporation and Grumman Corporation in 1994.

453.

Northrop Corporation was founded by Jack Northrop in 1939 as a successor to his previous companies, focusing on innovative aircraft design.

454.

Grumman Corporation was established in 1930 by Leroy Grumman and his partners, initially producing amphibious aircraft known as "Grumman Cats."

455.

Northrop's early designs included the YB-35 and YB-49 flying wing bombers, which were innovative for their time but faced technical challenges.

456.

Grumman gained recognition for producing iconic aircraft like the F4F Wildcat and TBF Avenger during World War II.

457.

One of Northrop's notable successes was the development of the P-61 Black Widow, a night fighter aircraft used during World War II.

458.

The merger of Northrop and Grumman created a diversified aerospace and defense company with capabilities spanning from aircraft to space systems.

459.

Northrop Grumman's technologies are used in a wide range of applications, including military aircraft, space exploration, cybersecurity, and more.

460.

The company played a crucial role in the Apollo program, producing the Lunar Module that landed astronauts on the moon.

461.

Northrop Grumman's contributions to space exploration continued with the development of the James Webb Space Telescope, a successor to the Hubble Space Telescope.

462.

The B-2 Spirit stealth bomber, known as the "Spirit of Innovation," is one of Northrop Grumman's most iconic creations, showcasing advanced aviation technology.

463.

The company's expertise extends to unmanned systems, including drones and autonomous vehicles used in various defense and civilian applications.

464.

Northrop Grumman's Electronic Systems sector specializes in developing advanced electronics and communication systems for military use.

465.

The company's Aerospace Systems sector focuses on designing and manufacturing aircraft, spacecraft, and related systems.

466.

Northrop Grumman's Information Systems sector provides solutions for cybersecurity, information technology, and defense systems integration.

467.

The company's Innovation Systems sector, formerly known as Orbital ATK, is involved in space launch vehicles, satellite systems, and more.

468.

Northrop Grumman's commitment to sustainability is evident through initiatives aimed at reducing its environmental impact and promoting clean energy.

469.

The company has been recognized for its diversity and inclusion efforts, earning a spot on DiversityInc's Top 50 Companies for Diversity list.

470.

Northrop Grumman's Advanced Technology Lab explores emerging technologies, such as artificial intelligence, quantum computing, and advanced materials.

471.

The company's history is intertwined with major historical events, including its contributions to the space race and Cold War defense efforts.

472.

Northrop Grumman's business operations extend beyond the United States, with offices and facilities around the world.

473.

The company is involved in various philanthropic initiatives, supporting education, veterans' causes, and STEM programs.

474.

Northrop Grumman's employees have a strong tradition of volunteerism, contributing to their local communities through service projects.

475.

The company's culture emphasizes innovation, collaboration, and a commitment to delivering mission-critical solutions to its customers.

476.

Northrop Grumman's technological advancements have contributed to the modernization of defense systems and capabilities.

477.

The company's Aerospace Systems sector is known for producing the Global Hawk unmanned surveillance aircraft and the Triton maritime surveillance UAV.

478.

Northrop Grumman has a legacy of supporting military readiness through the development of cutting-edge military platforms.

479.

The company's expertise in electronic warfare and radar systems plays a significant role in modern military operations.

480.

Northrop Grumman's focus on sustainability includes initiatives to reduce energy consumption, greenhouse gas emissions, and waste generation.

481.

The company is a major contributor to the defense industrial base, providing critical capabilities to national security efforts.

482.

Northrop Grumman's commitment to research and development has led to advancements in aerospace, defense, and technology sectors.

483.

The company's collaboration with government agencies and partners has resulted in innovative solutions to complex challenges.

484.

Northrop Grumman is recognized for its leadership in promoting cybersecurity best practices and solutions.

485.

The company's involvement in space exploration includes contributions to the Mars rover missions and other interplanetary exploration efforts.

486.

Northrop Grumman's workforce includes engineers, scientists, technologists, and experts in various fields.

487.

The company's legacy of innovation is built upon a foundation of technical excellence and a dedication to pushing the boundaries of what is possible.

488.

Northrop Grumman's corporate social responsibility initiatives extend to promoting STEM education and inspiring the next generation of innovators.

489.

The company's commitment to ethical business practices and integrity is reflected in its values and code of conduct.

490.

Northrop Grumman's history includes partnerships with other aerospace and defense companies, contributing to industry collaboration.

491.

The company's contributions to space-based capabilities include satellite systems, communication networks, and space situational awareness.

492.

Northrop Grumman's advanced sensor systems play a crucial role in national security, surveillance, and intelligence gathering.

493.

The company's aerospace innovations have influenced the design and development of modern military aircraft.

494.

Northrop Grumman's aerospace systems have applications beyond defense, including research, environmental monitoring, and disaster response.

495.

The company's legacy of pioneering aviation and space technologies continues to shape its role in advancing global security.

496.

Northrop Grumman's commitment to diversity is reflected in its leadership team, which includes individuals with diverse backgrounds and experiences.

497.

The company's support for veterans includes initiatives aimed at hiring, retaining, and recognizing the contributions of military personnel.

498.

Northrop Grumman's global presence allows it to collaborate with international partners and support global security efforts.

499.

The company's corporate responsibility extends to environmental stewardship, social impact, and governance practices.

500.

Northrop Grumman's ongoing dedication to innovation and technological advancement positions it as a key player in shaping the future of aerospace and defense industries.

501.

The Lockwood-Mathews Mansion, located in Norwalk, Connecticut, is a stunning example of Second Empire-style architecture.

502.

The mansion was designed by renowned architect Detlef Lienau and built between 1864 and 1868.

503.

The mansion was the primary residence of LeGrand Lockwood, a wealthy financier and railroad tycoon.

504.

LeGrand Lockwood was known as the "Lumber Baron of New York" due to his success in the timber industry.

505.

The mansion's construction cost around $2 million in 1868, which would be equivalent to approximately $38 million today.

506.

The mansion's exterior features a distinctive mansard roof, elaborate dormer windows, and intricate ironwork.

507.

The interior of the mansion boasts opulent decoration, including ornate plasterwork, carved woodwork, and marble fireplaces.

508.

The mansion has 62 rooms spread over four floors, with a total square footage of around 44,000 square feet.

509.

The mansion's grand hall is particularly impressive, with a soaring ceiling and a stunning spiral staircase.

510.

The mansion's architectural style is a blend of French Second Empire and Italianate influences.

511.

The mansion's dining room features intricately carved woodwork and a stunning fireplace.

512.

The mansion's library is adorned with hand-painted ceiling frescoes and floor-to-ceiling bookshelves.

513.

The mansion's ballroom is known for its exquisite crystal chandeliers and ornate plasterwork.

514.

The mansion was one of the first in the United States to have indoor plumbing and central heating.

515.

The mansion was equipped with an elevator, a cutting-edge technology of the time.

516.

The mansion's grounds originally included a large conservatory, gardens, and a carriage house.

517.

The mansion's conservatory was a lavish space with exotic plants, reflecting the Victorian fascination with botany.

518.

LeGrand Lockwood spared no expense when furnishing the mansion with imported European furniture and art.

519.

The mansion's original art collection included pieces by renowned artists such as Frederic Church and Albert Bierstadt.

520.

LeGrand Lockwood tragically died in 1872, just four years after the mansion's completion, leaving his wife, Ann, and their children.

521.

Following Lockwood's death, the mansion changed hands several times and underwent various modifications.

522.

The mansion served as the clubhouse for the Norwalk YMCA from 1926 to 1938.

523.

In 1941, the City of Norwalk purchased the mansion and surrounding property to use as a park.

524.

The mansion was designated a National Historic Landmark in 1971 for its architectural and historical significance.

525.

The Friends of the Lockwood-Mathews Mansion Museum was established in 1966 to restore and preserve the mansion.

526.

The mansion has been featured in several films and television shows, including "Dark Shadows."

527.

The mansion is known for its paranormal activity, and ghost tours and investigations are popular among visitors.

528.

The Lockwood-Mathews Mansion Museum offers guided tours that provide insights into the mansion's history and architecture.

529.

The mansion's collections include period furniture, decorative arts, clothing, and artifacts that showcase the Victorian era.

530.

The mansion's preservation efforts have helped maintain its original grandeur and historical significance.

531.

The mansion is a popular venue for weddings, special events, and cultural programs.

532.

The mansion's stunning exterior has made it a favorite subject for photographers and artists.

533.

The mansion's beautiful gardens have been restored to their Victorian-era splendor.

534.

The mansion hosts educational programs, lectures, and exhibits that explore various aspects of Victorian life.

535.

The Lockwood-Mathews Mansion Museum is a prominent cultural institution in Fairfield County, Connecticut.

536.

The mansion's grand staircase features intricately carved banisters and newel posts.

537.

The mansion's drawing room showcases detailed ceiling frescoes and elegant furnishings.

538.

The mansion's music room is adorned with ornate plasterwork and features a grand piano.

539.

The mansion's second-floor bedrooms have period-appropriate furniture and decor.

540.

The mansion's third floor once housed servants' quarters, reflecting the social dynamics of the time.

541.

The mansion's tower offers panoramic views of the surrounding area and Long Island Sound.

542.

The mansion's construction materials included brownstone, brick, and a wooden frame.

543.

The mansion's original gas lighting fixtures have been preserved as part of its historical authenticity.

544.

The mansion's architectural design incorporates both symmetry and asymmetry, creating a visually appealing facade.

545.

The mansion's restoration work has involved careful research to ensure accuracy in period-appropriate detailing.

546.

The mansion's historical significance extends beyond its architectural beauty to its role in local and regional history.

547.

The mansion's ongoing maintenance and restoration efforts require continuous fundraising and community support.

548.

The mansion's history reflects the opulence of the Gilded Age and the aspirations of its wealthy owners.

549.

The Lockwood-Mathews Mansion remains a testament to the craftsmanship and innovation of the 19th century.

550.

The mansion's preservation and continued use as a museum contribute to the cultural enrichment of the local community and beyond.

551.

The Othniel C. Marsh House is located in New Haven, Connecticut, and is also known as the "Marsh Botanical Garden."

552.

The house was built in 1878 and was the former residence of Othniel Charles Marsh, a renowned American paleontologist.

553.

Othniel C. Marsh is famous for his contributions to the field of paleontology, particularly his rivalry with Edward Drinker Cope, known as the "Bone Wars."

554.

The house served as both a residence and a workspace for Marsh, where he conducted his scientific research and stored his fossil collections.

555.

The house is designed in the Second Empire architectural style, featuring a mansard roof, ornate dormers, and elaborate ironwork.

556.

The Marsh House is situated on the grounds of Yale University, where Marsh was a professor and curator at the Peabody Museum of Natural History.

557.

The house has a prominent tower that offers views of the surrounding area and the Yale University campus.

558.

The Marsh House is surrounded by beautifully landscaped gardens and greenhouses, which were used for Marsh's botanical research.

559.

Marsh used the grounds to cultivate a diverse collection of plants from around the world, creating a living laboratory for his studies.

560.

The Marsh Botanical Garden is one of the oldest university botanical gardens in the United States.

561.

The garden features a wide range of plant species, including tropical, subtropical, and temperate plants.

562.

The Marsh House and its botanical garden played a significant role in Marsh's scientific studies, allowing him to investigate plant evolution alongside his paleontological work.

563.

The house's interior includes a library, laboratory spaces, and living quarters where Marsh conducted his research and entertained fellow scientists.

564.

Marsh's research at the house contributed to advancements in the understanding of vertebrate evolution and the history of life on Earth.

565.

The house also served as a gathering place for Marsh's colleagues and students, fostering collaboration and scientific discussions.

566.

The Marsh House has been designated a National Historic Landmark due to its significance in the history of science.

567.

Today, the Marsh Botanical Garden continues to serve as a research and educational facility, focusing on plant conservation and environmental studies.

568.

The garden features several greenhouses, each with specific temperature and humidity conditions to support different plant species.

569.

The Marsh House showcases artifacts and memorabilia related to Othniel C. Marsh's life and scientific contributions.

570.

The Marsh House offers guided tours and educational programs that highlight the history of the property and its role in scientific research.

571.

The house's connection to Yale University makes it a valuable resource for students and researchers studying botany, paleontology, and history of science.

572.

The Marsh Botanical Garden's mission includes promoting the understanding of plants' significance in human culture and ecosystems.

573.

The garden's collections include rare and endangered plant species, contributing to efforts in plant conservation.

574.

The Marsh House and its botanical garden provide a tranquil and educational environment for visitors interested in science and nature.

575.

The house's architecture reflects the Victorian-era aesthetic, characterized by its intricate detailing and ornamentation.

576.

The Marsh House stands as a testament to the importance of preserving historical landmarks that have played a pivotal role in scientific discovery.

577.

The garden's research efforts extend to areas such as plant ecology, genetics, and biodiversity.

578.

The Marsh Botanical Garden is open to the public, offering a place for visitors to explore diverse plant life and learn about scientific research.

579.

The Marsh House has been featured in documentaries and educational programs, highlighting its role in scientific history.

580.

The house's location on the Yale campus makes it easily accessible to students and researchers interested in botany and paleontology.

581.

The Marsh Botanical Garden is involved in outreach programs, engaging with local schools and communities to promote plant science education.

582.

The garden's educational activities include workshops, lectures, and exhibits that connect visitors with the world of plants and scientific discovery.

583.

The Marsh House represents the legacy of Othniel C. Marsh, who significantly contributed to the understanding of Earth's history and evolution.

584.

The garden's collections encompass a wide range of plant families, showcasing the diversity and complexity of plant life.

585.

The Marsh Botanical Garden's historical and scientific significance extends beyond its local impact to its broader contributions to botanical research.

586.

The house's architecture and design offer insights into the aesthetics of the Victorian era and the tastes of prominent scientists of the time.

587.

The Marsh House and its botanical garden provide a serene and contemplative environment for those interested in nature and scientific exploration.

588.

The garden's plant collections are organized in ways that highlight their evolutionary relationships and ecological adaptations.

589.

The Marsh Botanical Garden's dedication to plant conservation aligns with contemporary efforts to protect biodiversity and natural habitats.

590.

The house's historical value lies not only in its association with Othniel C. Marsh but also in its role as a center of scientific activity.

591.

The garden's horticultural practices encompass a wide range of techniques, from traditional gardening to modern methods of cultivation.

592.

The Marsh House and its surroundings offer a unique juxtaposition of scientific exploration and architectural beauty.

593.

The garden's emphasis on education and research makes it a valuable asset for fostering interest in botany and related fields.

594.

The house's connection to Yale University underscores the importance of academic institutions in advancing scientific knowledge.

595.

The Marsh Botanical Garden's contributions to plant science extend to areas such as plant physiology, genetics, and molecular biology.

596.

The Marsh House's historical significance is acknowledged by its inclusion on the National Register of Historic Places.

597.

The garden's role in plant research helps address contemporary challenges related to climate change and habitat loss.

598.

The house's location within the Yale campus makes it part of a larger educational and scientific community.

599.

The Marsh Botanical Garden's commitment to conservation aligns with global efforts to protect and preserve plant species.

600.

The Marsh House stands as a symbol of the intersection between scientific discovery, botanical exploration, and historical preservation.

601.

The grey seal (Halichoerus grypus) is one of the largest seal species and is found in the North Atlantic Ocean.

602.

Grey seals are known for their distinctive V-shaped nostrils and large, soulful eyes.

603.

They are highly intelligent marine mammals and are often curious about their surroundings.

604.

Grey seals have a varied coat color, ranging from light gray to almost black, and they often have dark spots and patterns on their bodies.

605.

Male grey seals are called bulls, and females are called cows. Young seals are referred to as pups.

606.

Grey seals are excellent swimmers and divers, capable of reaching depths of up to 600 feet (180 meters) and staying underwater for extended periods.

607.

They have specialized adaptations, including a streamlined body and strong flippers, that help them navigate through the water.

608.

Grey seals primarily feed on fish, including cod, herring, and flatfish. They are also known to eat crustaceans and squid.

609.

The diet of a grey seal can vary based on its location and the availability of prey species.

610.

Grey seals are skilled hunters, using their acute senses and excellent underwater vision to locate prey.

611.

During the breeding season, grey seals gather in large colonies on beaches, rocky shores, and remote islands.

612.

Grey seals give birth to their pups on land, and the mothers nurse their young for several weeks.

613.

Pupping season usually occurs between September and November.

614.

Newborn grey seal pups have soft, white fur called lanugo, which is eventually shed.

615.

Pups rely on their mother's milk, which is rich in fat, for nourishment during the critical early weeks of life.

616.

After the nursing period, grey seal pups are weaned and start to learn how to swim and catch their own food.

617.

Grey seals have an interesting vocal repertoire, including grunts, growls, and barks, which they use to communicate with each other.

618.

Adult male grey seals have a unique vocalization called a "roar" that they use to establish dominance and attract females.

619.

Grey seals have a lifespan of around 30-40 years, although some individuals can live longer.

620.

Grey seal populations are classified into two main subspecies: the Western Atlantic population and the Eastern Atlantic population.

621.

The Eastern Atlantic population is the larger of the two and is found along the coasts of Europe, including the UK and Ireland.

622.

Grey seals have a unique molting process, where they shed their old fur and grow new, waterproof fur to stay insulated in the cold water.

623.

They are well adapted to cold temperatures, with a layer of blubber under their skin that helps them stay warm.

624.

Grey seals are known for their playful behavior, often seen surfing in waves and interacting with each other in the water.

625.

They are also known to use their flippers to "wave" or slap the water's surface as a form of communication or play.

626.

Grey seals are protected by various laws and regulations in many countries to ensure their conservation.

627.

Historically, grey seals were hunted for their meat, blubber, and hides. However, modern conservation efforts have led to restrictions on hunting.

628.

Grey seals face various threats, including entanglement in fishing gear, habitat degradation, pollution, and climate change.

629.

Climate change can impact their prey availability and also affect their breeding sites due to rising sea levels and changing ice patterns.

630.

Conservation organizations work to monitor grey seal populations, address threats, and promote public awareness about these animals.

631.

Grey seals are a crucial part of marine ecosystems, playing a role in maintaining the balance of fish populations.

632.

They are considered apex predators, meaning they are at the top of the food chain in their marine habitats.

633.

Grey seals can be observed in their natural habitat by joining guided wildlife tours in areas where they are known to frequent.

634.

The seal's scientific name, Halichoerus grypus, is derived from Greek words meaning "hook-nosed sea pig."

635.

Grey seals are known to have a strong sense of smell, which helps them locate prey underwater.

636.

Their whiskers, called vibrissae, are highly sensitive and aid in detecting movements and vibrations in the water.

637.

Grey seals are known to have a hierarchy within their colonies, with dominant individuals having access to prime breeding and resting sites.

638.

Pup mortality rates can be high, with natural predation and environmental factors contributing to the survival of the fittest.

639.

The relationship between grey seals and humans has evolved over time, from being hunted to being admired and protected.

640.

Some grey seal colonies have become popular ecotourism destinations, offering opportunities for people to observe these animals in their natural habitat.

641.

The grey seal's ability to dive to great depths has intrigued researchers and led to studies on their physiological adaptations to pressure changes.

642.

Grey seals are known to travel long distances in search of food, sometimes covering hundreds of miles during their migrations.

643.

In recent years, advancements in tracking technology have allowed researchers to gain valuable insights into the movement patterns of grey seals.

644.

The growth rate of grey seal pups is impressive, with some doubling their birth weight in just a few weeks.

645.

Grey seals play a significant role in the cultural heritage of coastal communities, often being celebrated through art, literature, and folklore.

646.

Grey seals are known to exhibit curiosity towards humans in their aquatic environment, occasionally approaching divers and swimmers.

647.

They have an acute sense of hearing, which aids in detecting both underwater sounds and calls from other seals.

648.

Grey seals have evolved specialized adaptations to thrive in both aquatic and terrestrial environments.

649.

Their hind flippers are movable, which allows them to maneuver on land, and their front flippers are powerful tools for swimming.

650.

The conservation efforts dedicated to grey seals serve as a reminder of the interconnectedness of marine ecosystems and the importance of protecting these creatures for future generations.

651.

The grey wolf (Canis lupus) is one of the most widely distributed and recognized carnivores in the world.

652.

Grey wolves belong to the Canidae family, which includes dogs, foxes, and other canines.

653.

They have a diverse range of coat colors, including shades of gray, brown, black, and white, depending on their geographic location.

654.

Grey wolves are known for their social nature and complex pack structures.

655.

Packs typically consist of a dominant breeding pair, their offspring, and other subordinate members.

656.

Communication within wolf packs is crucial, involving a variety of vocalizations, body postures, and facial expressions.

657.

Howls are a significant means of communication among wolves, helping them locate each other over long distances.

658.

Grey wolves have an impressive sense of smell, which they use for tracking prey and communicating with other wolves.

659.

The size of wolf packs can vary depending on factors like prey availability and territory size.

660.

Wolves are opportunistic predators, feeding on a variety of animals including deer, elk, moose, smaller mammals, and even carrion.

661.

They are apex predators, playing a vital role in maintaining the health and balance of ecosystems by controlling prey populations.

662.

Wolves are highly adaptable, inhabiting a range of environments from forests and tundra to deserts and grasslands.

663.

The grey wolf's historical range covered much of North America, Europe, and Asia, but habitat loss and human activity have reduced their distribution.

664.

Wolves are known for their teamwork during hunts, where they use tactics to outsmart and catch prey.

665.

Wolf packs are known to establish territories that they defend against rival packs.

666.

Grey wolves have a gestation period of about 63 days, after which a litter of pups is born.

667.

Pups are usually born blind and deaf and rely on their mother's care for several weeks.

668.

Wolf pups start to eat regurgitated food from adult pack members when they are around 3 weeks old.

669.

The social structure within wolf packs helps with pup-rearing, as other pack members assist in providing food and protection.

670.

Wolves have a strong sense of family and pack loyalty, often working together to care for the young and old members.

671.

They have a wide vocal repertoire, including growls, barks, whines, and howls, each with distinct meanings.

672.

Grey wolves have historically been both revered and feared by humans, featuring prominently in many cultural myths and stories.

673.

Wolves play an essential role in Indigenous cultures and spiritual beliefs around the world.

674.

Despite their ecological importance, grey wolves have faced persecution due to conflicts with livestock and fear.

675.

Conservation efforts have helped protect and reintroduce wolf populations in some areas, leading to a better understanding of their ecological importance.

676.

The grey wolf's natural enemies include larger predators like bears and mountain lions, but human activity poses the most significant threat.

677.

Wolves have specialized adaptations for hunting, including strong jaws, sharp teeth, and excellent night vision.

678.

The grey wolf is closely related to domestic dogs, and through selective breeding, dogs were domesticated from wolves.

679.

In some cultures, the wolf symbolizes intelligence, freedom, and wildness.

680.

Wolves have a significant role in the concept of trophic cascades, where changes in predator populations can affect entire ecosystems.

681.

Grey wolves can travel long distances in search of food, often covering many miles in a day.

682.

Their powerful jaws and sharp teeth allow them to crush bones, making them capable of consuming even large prey in its entirety.

683.

Wolf packs are known to establish dens for raising pups, often located in remote areas for protection.

684.

In colder climates, grey wolves have a dense double coat that helps insulate them from harsh weather conditions.

685.

The size of a grey wolf can vary depending on geographic location, with some subspecies being larger than others.

686.

The decline of wolves in many regions led to the loss of their ecosystem-stabilizing effects, which has prompted efforts to reintroduce them.

687.

Grey wolves are monogamous and often mate for life, with the dominant breeding pair being the primary reproducing individuals within a pack.

688.

Wolf populations have faced challenges due to habitat fragmentation, road mortalities, and conflicts with humans.

689.

The International Wolf Center and other organizations work to educate the public about wolves and their ecological importance.

690.

Wolves play a vital role in controlling herbivore populations, which in turn affects plant communities and the balance of ecosystems.

691.

Wolf howls can carry for miles, and researchers can use their vocalizations to estimate population numbers and distribution.

692.

The grey wolf has been featured in literature, art, and movies as a symbol of both fear and admiration.

693.

Wolves can travel at speeds of up to 35 miles per hour (56 kilometers per hour) in short bursts.

694.

In some Native American cultures, wolves are seen as spirit guides and symbols of loyalty, family, and community.

695.

The grey wolf's scientific name, Canis lupus, reflects its connection to the broader canine family.

696.

Wolves have evolved a unique hierarchy within their packs, with an alpha male and female taking on leadership roles.

697.

The population status of grey wolves varies globally, with some regions experiencing recovery and others still facing threats.

698.

The conservation status of grey wolves is often influenced by political and cultural factors, as well as habitat protection efforts.

699.

Wolves are known for their intricate facial expressions, which they use to communicate dominance, submission, and emotions within the pack.

700.

The ongoing efforts to conserve and protect grey wolf populations highlight the importance of preserving apex predators and the complex ecosystems they inhabit.

701.

BP, originally known as the Anglo-Persian Oil Company, was founded in 1908 by William Knox D'Arcy.

702.

The company was established to explore and develop oil fields in Persia (now Iran), after D'Arcy acquired a concession from the Iranian government.

703.

The Anglo-Persian Oil Company discovered significant oil reserves in the Middle East, leading to its rapid growth and expansion.

704.

In 1914, the British government acquired a majority share in the company to secure oil supplies for the Royal Navy during World War I.

705.

The company's first oil well, known as Masjid-i-Suleiman, was drilled in 1908 and marked the beginning of oil exploration in the Middle East.

706.

In 1935, the company was renamed the Anglo-Iranian Oil Company (AIOC) to reflect its focus on Iranian oil resources.

707.

The AIOC played a crucial role in the global oil industry, with its Iranian oil supplying a significant portion of the world's demand.

708.

In 1951, Iran's Prime Minister Mohammad Mossadegh nationalized the Iranian oil industry, leading to a major crisis known as the Iranian Oil Crisis.

709.

The nationalization of the oil industry in Iran led to the temporary shutdown of the AIOC's operations in the country.

710.

In response to the crisis, the British government and the AIOC worked together to impose an international embargo on Iranian oil exports.

711.

The crisis was eventually resolved in 1954 through negotiations, and the company resumed operations in Iran.

712.

In 1954, the AIOC was renamed the British Petroleum Company, reflecting its broader international activities beyond Iran.

713.

BP expanded its operations to various parts of the world, including the North Sea, Alaska, and Africa, in addition to its operations in the Middle East.

714.

BP's logo, the green and yellow sunburst, was introduced in 1979 as a symbol of energy and sustainability.

715.

The 1970s marked a period of increased global energy demand and higher oil prices, which benefited oil-producing companies like BP.

716.

In 1987, BP acquired the U.S.-based oil company Standard Oil of Ohio (Sohio), expanding its presence in the United States.

717.

The Exxon Valdez oil spill in 1989 highlighted the environmental risks associated with oil transportation, prompting increased scrutiny of the oil industry.

718.

In 1997, BP merged with Amoco, creating BP Amoco plc, one of the largest energy companies in the world.

719.

The merger allowed BP to expand its operations and access new reserves in the United States.

720.

In 2000, BP Amoco plc was renamed BP plc to reflect its unified global identity.

721.

BP made significant investments in renewable energy sources and alternative technologies, aiming to diversify its energy portfolio.

722.

The Deepwater Horizon oil spill in 2010, one of the largest environmental disasters in history, had a profound impact on BP's reputation and finances.

723.

The oil spill led to legal battles, environmental damage, and significant financial liabilities for BP.

724.

In the aftermath of the Deepwater Horizon disaster, BP committed to improving safety measures and enhancing environmental stewardship.

725.

BP's Beyond Petroleum campaign aimed to position the company as a leader in sustainable energy solutions.

726.

BP's involvement in renewable energy included investments in solar, wind, and biofuels, although these efforts remained a small part of its overall business.

727.

BP rebranded itself as "Beyond Petroleum" in 2000, highlighting its commitment to clean energy and environmental responsibility.

728.

BP has been involved in various environmental initiatives, including reducing carbon emissions and investing in carbon capture and storage technologies.

729.

The company faced criticism for its continued reliance on fossil fuels despite its renewable energy initiatives.

730.

In 2020, BP announced a new strategy to transform into a net-zero emissions company by 2050, focusing on reducing carbon emissions from its operations.

731.

BP's net-zero emissions strategy involves increasing investments in renewable energy, reducing oil and gas production, and carbon offset initiatives.

732.

BP's long-standing CEO, Lord Browne, played a pivotal role in shaping the company's modern image and strategic direction.

733.

BP has faced controversies related to human rights issues, environmental accidents, and its corporate practices in different parts of the world.

734.

The company has also faced legal battles and lawsuits related to various environmental and safety incidents.

735.

BP's operations cover various aspects of the energy industry, including exploration, production, refining, marketing, and distribution of oil and gas products.

736.

The company's upstream activities involve exploration and production of oil and gas reserves, while downstream activities focus on refining and marketing.

737.

BP operates in more than 70 countries and employs thousands of people worldwide.

738.

BP's corporate headquarters is located in London, United Kingdom.

739.

The energy industry's volatility, changing regulations, and market dynamics have influenced BP's financial performance over the years.

740.

BP has invested in research and development to enhance its technological capabilities in oil exploration, drilling, and energy production.

741.

The company has been involved in various philanthropic initiatives, contributing to education, health, and environmental causes.

742.

BP's partnership with the University of California, Berkeley, led to the creation of the Energy Biosciences Institute, focusing on advanced biofuels and alternative energy sources.

743.

BP's involvement in joint ventures and partnerships with other energy companies and governments has been a significant aspect of its business strategy.

744.

BP has been recognized for its efforts to improve safety standards and operational practices in the oil and gas industry.

745.

The company's financial performance has been influenced by fluctuating oil prices, geopolitical factors, and global economic conditions.

746.

BP's presence in various countries has allowed it to contribute to local economies and create employment opportunities.

747.

The transition to renewable energy sources and the reduction of carbon emissions present both challenges and opportunities for BP's future business strategy.

748.

BP has been ranked on various lists of the world's largest and most influential energy companies.

749.

The company's commitment to sustainability and environmental responsibility has shaped its approach to business decisions and operations.

750.

As of my knowledge cutoff date in September 2021, BP continues to navigate the challenges of the evolving energy landscape while pursuing its net-zero emissions goal and contributing to the global energy transition. Please note that there may have been developments or changes since that time.

751.

Honeywell's roots can be traced back to 1885 when inventor Albert Butz patented the furnace regulator and alarm.

752.

The company was originally named "Butz Thermo-Electric Regulator Co." and was focused on creating heating controls.

753.

In 1927, the company merged with the Minneapolis Heat Regulator Company, forming Minneapolis-Honeywell Regulator Co.

754.

Honeywell played a significant role during World War II, producing technologies for the military, including guidance and control systems.

755.

Honeywell's first computer, the Honeywell H316, was introduced in 1966 as a minicomputer designed for scientific and engineering computations.

756.

The company's nickname, "The Round," originated from the iconic circular thermostat design introduced in the 1950s.

757.

Honeywell expanded its product range to include aerospace systems, automotive products, and home automation technologies.

758.

The "Black Box" flight data recorder, critical for aviation safety, was developed by Honeywell in the 1950s.

759.

Honeywell's first digital computer, the H200, was introduced in 1964 and marked a significant advancement in computing technology.

760.

Honeywell played a vital role in the Apollo moon landing missions by providing guidance and navigation systems for the spacecraft.

761.

In 1970, the company's name changed to Honeywell Inc., reflecting its broader range of products and services.

762.

Honeywell introduced the first all-digital flight management system in the 1980s, enhancing aircraft navigation and safety.

763.

The 1990s saw Honeywell expand into automation and control systems for industries like oil and gas, chemicals, and manufacturing.

764.

In 1999, Honeywell announced a merger with General Electric (GE), but the merger was blocked by regulatory authorities.

765.

Honeywell's acquisition of AlliedSignal in 1999 helped diversify its portfolio and establish its presence in aerospace and defense industries.

766.

Honeywell's "Connected Building" technologies enable smart and energy-efficient management of commercial and residential spaces.

767.

The company's Environmental and Combustion Controls business produces energy-efficient thermostats, heating, and ventilation systems.

768.

Honeywell's Turbocharger technologies enhance engine efficiency and performance in automotive and industrial applications.

769.

Honeywell has developed advanced technologies for aerospace, including cockpit systems, avionics, engines, and safety systems.

770.

The company's "UOP" division specializes in refining, petrochemical, and gas processing technologies.

771.

Honeywell's Quantum Solutions division focuses on the development of quantum computers for solving complex problems.

772.

Honeywell's "Safety and Productivity Solutions" segment provides solutions for industrial safety, supply chain, and productivity enhancement.

773.

The company's "Honeywell Forge" platform leverages data analytics and AI to optimize industrial operations.

774.

Honeywell's commitment to sustainability is reflected in its efforts to develop eco-friendly products and reduce its environmental footprint.

775.

The company has been recognized for its efforts in diversity, equity, and inclusion, receiving accolades for workplace diversity.

776.

Honeywell has a long history of innovation, with over 150 years of technological advancements.

777.

The company has a global presence, with operations in more than 70 countries and customers in various industries.

778.

Honeywell has a strong emphasis on research and development, investing significantly in cutting-edge technologies.

779.

The Honeywell Aerospace division produces aircraft engines, avionics, and electronic systems for commercial and military applications.

780.

The company's "Intelligrated" division specializes in automation solutions for warehousing, distribution, and e-commerce operations.

781.

Honeywell's "Resideo" division focuses on providing smart home solutions, including security, comfort, and energy management.

782.

Honeywell's "Life Care Solutions" offers medical devices and technologies for patient monitoring and healthcare facilities.

783.

The Honeywell Foundation supports various charitable initiatives, including education, disaster relief, and community development.

784.

The company's commitment to safety is evident in its products, which include gas detectors, fire alarms, and personal protective equipment.

785.

Honeywell's "AIDC" division provides automatic identification and data capture solutions, including barcode scanners and mobile computers.

786.

The company's legacy of innovation is reflected in its numerous patents across a wide range of technologies.

787.

Honeywell's aerospace technologies have been instrumental in enhancing the safety and efficiency of air travel.

788.

The company's leadership in automation and control systems has transformed industries by improving productivity and operational efficiency.

789.

Honeywell has received numerous awards and recognitions for its technological advancements and contributions to various industries.

790.

The company's commitment to sustainability includes efforts to reduce greenhouse gas emissions, conserve resources, and promote renewable energy solutions.

791.

Honeywell's "Honeywell User Experience" (HUE) focuses on user-centric design principles to create intuitive and effective products.

792.

The company's commitment to ethical business practices is reflected in its values and corporate governance initiatives.

793.

Honeywell's involvement in space exploration extends beyond Earth, with technologies that have supported various space missions.

794.

The company's innovations have helped shape modern life, from everyday household products to complex industrial systems.

795.

Honeywell's digital transformation initiatives include leveraging the Industrial Internet of Things (IIoT) to optimize operations.

796.

The company's "Honeywell Ventures" division invests in emerging technologies and startups to drive innovation.

797.

Honeywell's "Performance Materials and Technologies" division provides advanced materials, catalysts, and process technologies for various industries.

798.

The company's commitment to safety extends to its industrial process solutions, which help manage risks and enhance operational safety.

799.

Honeywell's products and solutions have a global impact, enhancing the quality of life and contributing to economic growth.

800.

Honeywell's legacy as an innovator continues to influence the world through its technology-driven solutions across multiple industries.

801.

The Mashantucket Pequot Reservation Archaeological District is located in Ledyard, Connecticut, USA.

802.

The district covers an area of approximately 214 acres and is home to the Mashantucket Pequot Tribe.

803.

The Mashantucket Pequot Tribe is recognized as a federally recognized Native American tribe.

804.

The district has been listed on the National Register of Historic Places since 1988.

805.

The Mashantucket Pequot Tribe is known for their rich cultural heritage and history.

806.

The district contains various archaeological sites that provide insights into the history and culture of the Mashantucket Pequot people.

807.

The archaeological sites within the district span thousands of years, representing different periods of Native American history.

808.

The Pequot War of 1636-1637 was a significant event that impacted the Mashantucket Pequot Tribe and their land.

809.

The Foxwoods Resort Casino, operated by the Mashantucket Pequot Tribe, is situated within the district and is one of the largest casinos in the world.

810.

The district is part of the larger Mashantucket Pequot Reservation, which includes both developed and natural areas.

811.

Archaeological excavations within the district have revealed artifacts such as pottery, tools, and other items used by the tribe.

812.

The district has provided valuable information about the lifeways, traditions, and cultural practices of the Mashantucket Pequot people.

813.

The Mashantucket Pequot Museum and Research Center, located adjacent to the district, is a renowned institution that showcases the history and culture of the tribe.

814.

The museum features interactive exhibits, displays, and educational programs that offer visitors a deeper understanding of the Mashantucket Pequot Tribe.

815.

The Mashantucket Pequot Tribe has a strong commitment to preserving and sharing their cultural heritage.

816.

The district's archaeological sites have contributed to the broader understanding of Native American history in the region.

817.

The district's significance extends beyond archaeological and historical aspects, as it holds cultural and spiritual importance to the Mashantucket Pequot people.

818.

The Mashantucket Pequot Tribe has engaged in collaborations with archaeologists, researchers, and institutions to study and document their heritage.

819.

Traditional crafts, such as beadwork, pottery, and basketry, continue to be practiced by members of the Mashantucket Pequot Tribe.

820.

The district's archaeological sites include remnants of pre-contact Native American settlements, indicating long-term habitation.

821.

The Mashantucket Pequot Tribe's language, Pequot-Mohegan, is part of the Algonquian language family.

822.

The tribe's history involves resilience and adaptation in the face of challenges posed by European colonization.

823.

The Mashantucket Pequot Tribe has maintained their sovereignty and self-governance through their tribal government.

824.

The Mashantucket Pequot Reservation Archaeological District is situated in a picturesque landscape with forests and water bodies.

825.

The district's preservation efforts extend to both physical artifacts and intangible cultural practices.

826.

The tribe's traditional ceremonies, such as powwows, storytelling, and feasts, continue to be celebrated within the district.

827.

The district's archaeological sites have been instrumental in dispelling misconceptions and stereotypes about Native American cultures.

828.

The Mashantucket Pequot Tribe has worked to address cultural sensitivity and representation in both academia and public perceptions.

829.

Tribal members actively participate in cultural revitalization efforts, passing down knowledge and practices to younger generations.

830.

The district's archaeological resources have led to insights into the Mashantucket Pequot Tribe's interactions with neighboring tribes and European settlers.

831.

The Mashantucket Pequot Tribe's history reflects both their cultural resilience and the challenges posed by colonialism.

832.

The district's archaeological significance has led to its protection and recognition as a valuable cultural heritage site.

833.

The Mashantucket Pequot Tribe's sovereignty allows them to make decisions regarding the preservation and management of the district.

834.

The archaeological district's location provides a physical connection to the tribe's ancestral land.

835.

The Mashantucket Pequot Tribe's commitment to education and cultural sharing is evident in their collaborations with educational institutions.

836.

The district's archaeological sites offer valuable opportunities for archaeological research and learning.

837.

The Mashantucket Pequot Tribe actively engages with visitors, sharing their history, culture, and perspectives.

838.

The district's archaeological sites include evidence of trade networks and interactions with other indigenous communities.

839.

The Mashantucket Pequot Tribe has embraced modern technologies to connect with a wider audience and share their heritage.

840.

The Mashantucket Pequot Reservation Archaeological District is part of ongoing efforts to recognize and protect indigenous heritage.

841.

The district's significance reaches beyond regional boundaries, contributing to the broader understanding of Native American history and cultures.

842.

The Mashantucket Pequot Tribe's identity is deeply intertwined with the district's archaeological resources.

843.

The district's landscape and natural resources hold spiritual importance for the tribe.

844.

The Mashantucket Pequot Tribe has developed programs to involve youth in cultural preservation, fostering a sense of pride and connection.

845.

The district's archaeological sites have been used to illustrate the evolving lifestyles of the Mashantucket Pequot people.

846.

The Mashantucket Pequot Tribe's cultural center offers workshops, demonstrations, and performances to engage the public.

847.

The archaeological district serves as a reminder of the Mashantucket Pequot Tribe's enduring presence and contributions to the region.

848.

The district's protection and preservation align with the tribe's commitment to environmental stewardship.

849.

The Mashantucket Pequot Reservation Archaeological District is a testament to the resilience and perseverance of the Mashantucket Pequot people.

850.

The district's ongoing management and preservation efforts reflect the tribe's dedication to honoring their heritage and sharing it with future generations.

851.

The Stephen Tyng Mather Home is located in Darien, Connecticut, USA.

852.

The home is named after Stephen Tyng Mather, the first director of the National Park Service.

853.

Stephen Tyng Mather was instrumental in the establishment and development of the National Park Service in the United States.

854.

The home was designed by prominent architect Henry Bacon, who also designed the Lincoln Memorial in Washington, D.C.

855.

The architectural style of the Stephen Tyng Mather Home is Colonial Revival.

856.

The home was built in 1900 and was originally used as a summer residence for the Mather family.

857.

The home is situated on a beautiful and expansive property surrounded by gardens and greenery.

858.

The Stephen Tyng Mather Home is listed on the National Register of Historic Places.

859.

The home's design reflects the elegance and sophistication of the early 20th century.

860.

Stephen Tyng Mather was a successful businessman and conservationist who played a pivotal role in preserving and protecting America's national parks.

861.

Mather's efforts to create the National Park Service helped establish a unified approach to managing and conserving natural and cultural resources.

862.

The home's interior features period-appropriate furnishings, providing a glimpse into the lifestyle of the Mather family.

863.

The Stephen Tyng Mather Home serves as a reminder of Mather's dedication to conservation and his role in shaping the national park system.

864.

The home's architectural details, such as its columns and symmetrical design, are characteristic of the Colonial Revival style.

865.

The property's landscaping includes lush gardens, walkways, and mature trees, creating a serene and picturesque environment.

866.

The Stephen Tyng Mather Home has historical significance not only due to its association with Mather but also as a representation of architectural trends of the time.

867.

The Mather family often hosted gatherings and social events at the home, reflecting their status and prominence in society.

868.

The home's design incorporates elements of both formal and informal living spaces.

869.

Stephen Tyng Mather's advocacy for national parks stemmed from his love of the outdoors and his belief in the importance of preserving natural wonders.

870.

Mather's dedication to conservation earned him the nickname "Father of the National Parks."

871.

The home's location in Darien allows for a suburban retreat while remaining close to the city of New York.

872.

The Stephen Tyng Mather Home has been well-preserved over the years, maintaining its historic charm.

873.

The property's gardens offer a tranquil space for reflection and relaxation.

874.

The home's architecture reflects a desire to connect with America's colonial past while embracing modern amenities.

875.

The Stephen Tyng Mather Home showcases the influence of historical preservation on architectural styles during the early 20th century.

876.

The home's construction materials and craftsmanship are representative of the quality of architecture during its era.

877.

The National Park Service continues to honor Stephen Tyng Mather's legacy through its dedication to preserving natural and cultural resources.

878.

The Stephen Tyng Mather Home is an example of a private residence that embodies architectural and historical significance.

879.

Mather's vision for the National Park Service emphasized accessibility and enjoyment of natural landscapes for all Americans.

880.

The home's proximity to New York City made it a convenient getaway for the Mather family.

881.

The architectural details of the home, such as its dormer windows and decorative woodwork, contribute to its aesthetic appeal.

882.

The Stephen Tyng Mather Home offers a glimpse into the lifestyle and values of the early 20th century upper class.

883.

Mather's advocacy for national parks helped preserve iconic sites like the Grand Canyon, Yellowstone, and Sequoia National Park.

884.

The home's historical significance extends to its association with the broader conservation movement in the United States.

885.

The Stephen Tyng Mather Home reflects Mather's dedication to both urban and natural environments.

886.

The property's landscape design includes features that were popular during the Colonial Revival era, such as structured gardens.

887.

Mather's leadership within the National Park Service set the foundation for the agency's continued role in conservation and public enjoyment.

888.

The home's architectural symmetry and balanced proportions are characteristic of the Colonial Revival style.

889.

The Stephen Tyng Mather Home is a testament to the connections between architecture, history, and conservation.

890.

The home's preservation showcases the importance of recognizing and protecting places of historical significance.

891.

The property's location in Darien offers a serene and private retreat from the hustle and bustle of city life.

892.

The Stephen Tyng Mather Home serves as a tribute to Mather's dedication to the protection of America's natural wonders.

893.

The home's design embodies a sense of timeless elegance that continues to resonate with visitors.

894.

The Stephen Tyng Mather Home's historical value extends beyond its physical structure to the principles it represents.

895.

Mather's role in establishing the National Park Service helped lay the groundwork for the conservation movement in the United States.

896.

The home's architecture draws inspiration from early American colonial design while incorporating modern conveniences.

897.

The Stephen Tyng Mather Home highlights the symbiotic relationship between historical preservation and environmental conservation.

898.

The property's gardens provide a tranquil setting that complements the architectural aesthetics of the home.

899.

Mather's commitment to preserving natural spaces aligned with the ideals of the Progressive Era.

900.

The Stephen Tyng Mather Home stands as a symbol of Mather's enduring legacy in shaping the preservation and enjoyment of America's national parks.

901.

Grivet monkeys, also known as Chlorocebus aethiops, are medium-sized primates belonging to the Old World monkey family.

902.

They are native to various regions of Africa, including the Sahel region, East Africa, and parts of the Arabian Peninsula.

903.

Grivet monkeys are easily recognized by their distinctive appearance, featuring a light olive-green to grayish coat and a white tuft of hair on their chin.

904.

The grivet monkey's scientific name, Chlorocebus aethiops, translates to "green monkey from Ethiopia," although they are found in various African countries.

905.

Grivets are known for their agility and adaptability, which has allowed them to inhabit a wide range of habitats, including grasslands, savannas, and forests.

906.

These monkeys have a complex social structure and live in groups called troops, which can consist of around 10 to 50 individuals.

907.

Grivets have a hierarchical social order within their troops, with dominant males having priority access to food and mates.

908.

They are diurnal animals, meaning they are active during the day and rest at night.

909.

Grivets are omnivorous, with their diet consisting of a variety of foods, including fruits, leaves, flowers, insects, and small vertebrates.

910.

They have specialized cheek pouches that allow them to store and carry food while foraging.

911.

Grivet monkeys are skilled climbers, using their prehensile tails and strong limbs to navigate through trees.

912.

Their long tails help them maintain balance while leaping from branch to branch.

913.

Grivets are known for their vocalizations, which include various calls, barks, and grunts that serve to communicate within the troop.

914.

Mothers and infants have a close bond, and the mother carries her young on her belly for the first few weeks of life.

915.

Grivets have excellent vision and depth perception, which aids in their arboreal lifestyle.

916.

They are also known to use grooming as a social bonding activity within the troop.

917.

In addition to vocalizations, they communicate through body language, such as grooming, gestures, and facial expressions.

918.

Grivet monkeys have a relatively long lifespan in the wild, often reaching around 20 years.

919.

They have a keen sense of smell, which helps them locate food sources and avoid predators.

920.

Grivets are susceptible to various predators, including large birds of prey, big cats, and humans.

921.

Habitat loss due to deforestation and human activity poses a significant threat to grivet populations.

922.

Some African cultures consider grivet monkeys sacred or bring them into local folklore and traditions.

923.

In certain regions, grivet monkeys have been used in medical research due to their close genetic relation to humans.

924.

These monkeys play a crucial role in ecosystems by aiding in seed dispersal and contributing to the health of plant populations.

925.

Grivets have a distinct grooming behavior known as "anting," where they rub or apply ants or other insects onto their fur to help manage parasites.

926.

In some areas, grivets are considered agricultural pests as they may raid crops.

927.

They are also known to adapt to urban environments, where they scavenge for food and interact with human settlements.

928.

Grivet monkeys are often kept as pets, though this practice is discouraged due to their complex social and environmental needs.

929.

They are agile swimmers and may enter water to cross rivers or access food.

930.

Grivet monkeys have a relatively small home range, usually limited to a few square kilometers.

931.

These monkeys are known to engage in play behavior, which helps them develop social and cognitive skills.

932.

Grivets are part of the guenon group of monkeys, which is characterized by their colorful and varied coats.

933.

They have cheek pouches that allow them to store food temporarily and eat it later when they find a safe location.

934.

Grivets are important to the ecosystem as they help control insect populations and disperse seeds of various plant species.

935.

In some cultures, grivet monkeys are considered symbols of fertility and luck.

936.

These monkeys are well-adapted to both hot and arid environments as well as more humid and tropical regions.

937.

Grivets are known for their curiosity and may investigate new objects or changes in their environment.

938.

In ancient Egyptian art and culture, grivet monkeys were sometimes depicted and held symbolic meanings.

939.

They have a robust grooming ritual that helps maintain social bonds and removes parasites from their fur.

940.

Grivets have a remarkable ability to adapt to changing environments and exploit new food sources.

941.

Their gestation period is around five to six months, and they usually give birth to a single offspring.

942.

Grivets are known to exhibit territorial behavior to defend their food sources and preferred sleeping sites.

943.

They are highly intelligent animals, capable of problem-solving and learning from their experiences.

944.

Grivets have forward-facing eyes that provide binocular vision, helping them accurately judge distances in their arboreal habitat.

945.

Some grivet populations have been negatively impacted by the pet trade, leading to their decline in the wild.

946.

These monkeys have complex vocalizations that help them communicate with other troop members over long distances.

947.

Grivets are vulnerable to diseases that affect primates, including infections and parasites.

948.

They are known to groom each other as a way of forming and reinforcing social bonds.

949.

Grivets play an essential role in their ecosystem by contributing to seed dispersal and pollination.

950.

Conservation efforts are crucial to protecting grivet monkeys and ensuring their survival in the wild, as habitat loss and other threats continue to impact their populations.

951.

Grizzly bears, scientifically known as Ursus arctos horribilis, are a subspecies of the brown bear and are native to North America.

952.

They are known for their distinctive hump of muscle on their shoulders, which supports their powerful front limbs.

953.

Grizzly bears have a wide range, from Alaska down to parts of Mexico and from the Pacific coast to the Great Plains.

954.

They are one of the largest land carnivores, with adult males weighing between 300 to 1,500 pounds (136 to 680 kg) and standing about 6 to 7 feet tall (1.8 to 2.1 meters) at the shoulder.

955.

Their fur can vary in color from blond to dark brown, and their coats are often highlighted with white-tipped fur.

956.

Grizzlies are omnivores, with a diet that includes plants, berries, grasses, insects, fish, small mammals, and carrion.

957.

During the summer and fall, they consume large amounts of food to build up fat reserves for hibernation.

958.

Grizzly bears are excellent swimmers and can cross rivers and lakes with ease.

959.

They have an incredible sense of smell, which they use to locate food, detect danger, and find potential mates.

960.

Grizzlies communicate through vocalizations such as growls, roars, and grunts, as well as body language like posturing and bluff charging.

961.

They are known to be solitary animals, with males and females coming together only during mating season.

962.

Female grizzlies are protective mothers, fiercely defending their cubs from potential threats.

963.

Cubs are usually born in the den during hibernation and are blind and helpless at birth.

964.

Grizzly bear cubs stay with their mothers for about two to three years, during which time they learn essential survival skills.

965.

Their lifespan in the wild can vary, but some grizzlies have been known to live up to 25-30 years.

966.

Grizzlies play a significant ecological role as seed dispersers, helping to spread the seeds of plants and contribute to forest health.

967.

They are considered a keystone species, meaning they have a disproportionate impact on their environment compared to their abundance.

968.

Grizzly bears are protected by law in many places due to their status as a threatened or endangered species.

969.

Their populations have declined historically due to habitat loss, hunting, and conflicts with humans.

970.

Grizzlies have a unique and complex mating ritual that can involve vocalizations, displays of dominance, and even playful behavior.

971.

During the breeding season, males mark their territory with scent markings and engage in confrontations with other males to establish dominance.

972.

Grizzlies are known for their digging skills and will often dig up the ground in search of roots, insects, or small mammals.

973.

They have a strong bite force and sharp claws that they use for digging, climbing, and hunting.

974.

Despite their size, grizzly bears are surprisingly fast runners and can reach speeds of up to 30 mph (48 km/h).

975.

Grizzlies have a unique method of hunting fish, known as "snorkeling," where they lower their heads into the water to catch fish with their mouths.

976.

They also have a hunting technique called "fishing weirs," where they build barriers in rivers to trap fish as the water recedes.

977.

Hibernation is a crucial survival strategy for grizzlies during the harsh winter months when food is scarce.

978.

During hibernation, their heart rate drops significantly, and they can go without eating or drinking for months.

979.

Grizzlies often seek out secluded dens in caves, hollowed-out trees, or dug-out spaces to give birth and hibernate.

980.

Their body temperature drops slightly during hibernation to conserve energy.

981.

Human-bear conflicts often arise when grizzlies are attracted to human food sources, leading to increased efforts to manage food waste in bear habitats.

982.

Grizzly bears have been a significant part of indigenous cultures for centuries, holding spiritual and cultural significance.

983.

They are featured in many native legends, stories, and art forms.

984.

The term "grizzly" comes from the appearance of their fur, which often has silver-tipped guard hairs that create a "grizzled" appearance.

985.

Despite their intimidating size and strength, many grizzly bears are quite shy and will avoid confrontation if possible.

986.

They have an intricate system of vocalizations and body language to communicate various emotions, intentions, and warnings.

987.

Grizzlies have a well-developed memory and can remember food sources, territories, and other bears for extended periods.

988.

In some places, grizzlies are known to engage in rubbing behaviors on trees, rocks, or the ground to mark their scent and communicate with other bears.

989.

Grizzlies are considered a flagship species for wilderness conservation, as their presence indicates a healthy and intact ecosystem.

990.

The protection and conservation of grizzly bears often involve efforts to safeguard their habitat and manage human interactions.

991.

Some national parks and protected areas are home to healthy grizzly populations, providing visitors with the opportunity to observe these magnificent creatures in their natural habitat.

992.

The Yellowstone National Park region is one of the most iconic grizzly bear habitats in the United States.

993.

Grizzlies have made a remarkable recovery in some areas due to conservation efforts and legal protections.

994.

Some organizations work to educate the public about coexisting with grizzly bears and reducing potential conflicts.

995.

In North America, the grizzly bear is featured on the California state flag, symbolizing the state's connection with wildlife and nature.

996.

Grizzly bears are known to have a profound influence on the ecosystems they inhabit, shaping vegetation patterns and influencing other species' behavior.

997.

They are excellent climbers and can ascend trees with relative ease.

998.

Grizzlies have been subjects of numerous studies aimed at understanding their behaviors, population dynamics, and interactions with humans.

999.

The film "Grizzly Man" directed by Werner Herzog tells the story of Timothy Treadwell, who lived among grizzly bears in Alaska for several years.

1000.

Grizzly bears continue to capture the fascination and respect of people around the world, highlighting the importance of conserving their habitats and coexisting harmoniously.